Even More

Remarkable Names

Tarantula Turner, Schoolgirl

Even More

Remarkable Names

Compiled & annotated by
John Train

Illustrations by Pierre Le-Tan
Foreword by Brendan Gill

Clarkson N. Potter, Inc., Publishers, New York
Distributed by Crown Publishers, Inc.

Published simultaneously in Canada by General Publishing Com-
pany Limited
First edition
Printed in the United States of America

*The portraits in this book are drawn entirely from my imagination
and are in no way intended to be considered as likenesses or
caricatures of the people named.*

—PIERRE LE-TAN

We welcome further nominations for a subsequent edition, always
with documentation. *They may be sent to the Office of Nomenclature Stabilization, Box 157, R.D. 2, Bedford, New York.*

Library of Congress Cataloging in Publication Data

Train, John.
  Even more remarkable names.

  1. Names, Personal—Anecdotes, facetiae, satire, etc.
I. Title.
CS2309.T7 1979   929.4   79–16185
ISBN 0–517–53694–3

To Ptah, who for the Egyptians "created the whole world and even the gods by uttering the name of each being or thing," and who should clearly be the patron of onomastics, the work is dedicated.

Ingeborg von Zitzewitz

FOREWORD

From our present vantage point in time, many people may find it difficult, looking back upon 1979, to comprehend how little known to fame John Train was at that period in our history. Laughable today to suppose that he could walk down Fifth Avenue as he did then, unaccompanied by cheering crowds, with few if any pretty girls hurling themselves to the ground in front of him and kissing his feet. Yet this was the case, and it is worthwhile our asking why. Perhaps these few words from one who knows the leader well may serve to provide an explanation.

To begin with, we must take care not to exaggerate the degree of Train's obscurity. Though born in a stable and brought up under troubled circumstances, by 1979 he had risen to be Chairman, President, and Chief Executive Officer of the Office of Nomenclatural Stabilization, already coming to be known among the plebs as ONOSTA. In all fairness, one must point out that ONOSTA wasn't then what it is today. Probably the simplest way to convey the difference, which is one of scale, is by means, or dint, of a physical analogy. (Our leader has always been strongly in favor of physical analogies. The few years that he spent behind bars in the early eighties were the result of an episode in which the physical unjustly received far more attention in the press — and in court — than the analogical. The girl herself received negligible injuries.)

To return to our muttons, our analogy, or, more precisely, our comparison may be stated in the following terms:

In 1979, ONOSTA occupied a simple steel and cinder-block building in Bedford, New York, which provided a scant two and three-quarters acres of office space. Today, the ONOSTA tower, designed by Paul Segal and I. M. Pei (a partnership formed in early 1980 and subsequently dissolved, by mutual consent), rises a full one hundred stories above Bedford. Nightly its windows pour hundreds of millions of candlepower of light over the adjacent community, where the inhabitants lie contentedly abed and repeat until the so-called "wee hours" (a Victorian bowdlerization of the more robust "wee-wee hours") the simple, heartfelt mantra "God bless our leader."

It was in that same annus mirabilis of 1979 that Train received the Nobel Prize for Onomastic Gymnastics from the hand of the King of Sweden. Still later in the year he was voted the Rose of Mooncoin at the annual County Sligo Bull and Ram Fair. Certain dry-as-dust scholiasts have since argued that "Rose" was a typographical error in the printed program for "ross," defined by the O.E.D. as "rubbish, refuse, dregs (first use, 1630)," and that our leader was, in actual fact, voted "Rubbish, Refuse, and Dregs of Mooncoin" on that happy occasion. Nonsense! There is no such word as "ross" in County Sligo, whatever may be the situation in nearby County Leitrim; "Rose" it is, and one may as well note in passing that the Irish peasantry has long found it hard to distinguish differences of gender, to say nothing of differences between species. (See Mitchell, J., Bestiality in the West, Doubleday & Company, 1982.)

This completes our explanation, which some may feel is

The Boring School

more exhaustive than absolutely necessary, of Train's early obscurity and contemporary fame. One word more: Could anything in the world be more obvious than that a preoccupation with remarkable names would be sure to characterize a child known to his closest intimates almost from the cradle as "Johnnie Choo-choo"?

—Brendan Gill

PREFACE

The Office of Nomenclature Stabilization has made the surprising discovery that what one might call the free-form nutty name—Oldmouse Waltz, Cashmere Tango Obedience, Eucalyptus Yoho—*is the one indigenous American art form. (Another contender, the totem pole, is also found in New Guinea, and is extinct here anyway; jazz, said to have originated in New Orleans funeral processions, is a combination of existing European and African elements.) Some foreign names, notably English, have a poetic ring; but almost never as a result of fantasy. In an English or Chinese name of the richer sort logic underlies every element, as in a heraldic device; it's not, as with* Odious Champagne *or* Fairy Clutter, *the free music of imagination.*

Take one of our favorites, a lumber dealer of Sandusky, Ohio, Mr. Humperdink Fangboner. *Dickens couldn't have done better. Like a good* Times *puzzle, the surprising parts produce a surprising whole.* Fangboner, *to start. Note the cutting edge, the spearhead:* Fang. *A clear warning—Don't Tread on Me. And the strength of the reinforcing* Bone. *Nothing supine or invertebrate there. It has the sinister force of Dickens's* Murdstone. *And even Dickens could not have outdone the sprightly yet harmonious overture:* Humperdink. *First, the ominous* Hump, *evoking the ship of the desert . . . tracks across the shifting dunes, whining houris, glowering sheiks, petrodollars; or the hump of the hunchback, conferring good fortune on whoever touches it; or indeed the erotic sense of* hump: *fevered couplings of camels, of hunchbacks . . . but enough. Then, the sprightly grace note of* Dink, *in, as it were,* allegro spiritoso *time, with its refreshing contrast to the somber weight of* Hump *and* Fang—*a spoonful of sherbet between two rich plates of a sumptuous banquet.*

And then, like the resolution of the primary and secondary themes of a symphony, the full Humperdink, *suggesting musical genius, Hansel and Gretel wandering in a wood . . . so fitting for one called by destiny to deal in the products of the forest. Finally the magnificent consummation, the whole orchestra,* tutti, fortissimo, *in C major:* HUMPERDINK FANGBONER. *A* recondita armonia *. . . evocative as a verse of Mallarmé, a haiku of Bashō.*

We find nothing comparable to these American fantasies in other cultures, except here and there in fiction. Dickens, to be sure, the Mozart of the funny names business, showed a marvelous power of onomastic invention, from Uriah Heep *to* Mr. Micawber, *but it fell to the New World to* plant its flag upon the heights to which, with a cry of "Excelsior!" he pointed the way. America, not old England, brought forth Katz Meow, Positive Wassermann Johnson, and T. Fud Pucker Tucker, just as so many of the visions of Jules Verne were first reduced to practice by the National Aeronautics and Space Administration.

We might observe in passing that the weird confections bestowed by many American families upon their infants are not as remote as one might think from the customs of an earlier day. Before the Norman Conquest the inhabitants of an English village would invent novel given names for each child that came along, like yachts or racehorses, so no family names were needed. Thus, only a handful of English kings before William the Conqueror bore the same name as any of their predecessors. (A similar effect is being sought today by the citizens of Florida.) However, after 1066 England's Norman masters required that all given names be drawn from a hagiology of about two hundred recognized saints, which meant that in all but the most modest hamlets, duplications became inevitable and surnames necessary.

America seems to be heading the other way, toward the elimination of surnames, particularly in the younger generation, who, one gathers, were devised by parthenogenesis, or perhaps in the lab, without paternal intervention. "Dad, this is Jennifer and Nicole." Parent, sotto voce: "Jennifer and Nicole who?" Child: "Huh?" As the family, and family names, expire, a broader repertoire of given names will be required for identification. The work of the Office will, we hope, push out the limits of the possible.

Our earlier compilation, Remarkable Names of Real

People, *elicited a surprising response—over a thousand communications, some containing entire collections of considerable merit, many with convincing documentation. We are most grateful. The sources of the printable ones—for multiple submissions, the first to arrive—are noted in the Acknowledgments. (We regret that all our correspondents could not be listed, but that would have consumed the entire volume: nearly every patient of Dr. E. Z. Filler, the dentist, and almost the entire customer list of Mr.* Never Fail, *the builder, were kind enough to write, and the same for many other entries.)*

For simplicity we have anglicized the foreign given names in the text. Immaculate Conception Finkelstein *is originally* Immaculada Concepciòn, *and so on.*

Our favorite submission was that of Mrs. Wilson, of Hewlett, New York, whose message ends as follows:

> *There was one name I came upon in the Nassau County telephone book. That is the only one I'd care to remember but of course I've forgotten it. It bordered on the pornographic. How any mother latched that first name on that last name, I couldn't imagine. I have no idea what either was. So stupid.*

We are holding a space in case lightning strikes.

Turning to the other highlights of the period since the previous collection, we are glad to report continued sound progress in most sectors. That evergreen source, the Florida Bureau of Vital Statistics at Jacksonville, has given its attention to twins and has verified the following pairs:

Comfort and Satisfy Bottom, Sisters

A.C. *and* D.C.; Bigamy *and* Larceny; Curly *and* Early; *and* Pete *and* Repeat. *We urge our correspondents not to overlook this area. (The Rev. Dr. Theall, of Catholic University, Washington, D.C., has bestowed a seemly offering:* Ivory *and* Ovary, *male twins from Chicago.)*

We had occasion to confer with the family of Halloween Buggage, *of New Orleans (named after her birth date), and were touched to learn of the arrival on the earthly as well as onomastic scene of* Easter Buggage, *whose birthday the reader can readily surmise. The Office extends its felicitations and its hopes for further achievements: perhaps a* Rosh Hashana Buggage (*Ross*) *can be followed by a* Michaelmas Buggage (*Mike*). *And if invention fails, we stand at the ready, our obstetrical bag packed, as ever* . . . *not with mere forceps and chloroform, but with our trusty microfiches and thesaurus.*

J. T.

Lotta Crap

ABDERAZZAQ S. ABDEULHAFAFEETH
  Fitchburg, Massachusetts
  (*Fitchburg Sentinel*)

AIDA QUATTLEBAUM*
  Westminster, California

ANIL G. SHITOLE†
  Rochester, New York

ARIZONA ZIPPER
  New York City
  (*Village Voice*)

ASA MINER‡
  Wakefield, Rhode Island

Compare Tosca Zerk, daughter of Oscar Zerk, inventor of the Zerk Auto Grease Gun, and Manon Lescaut Voightsburger.

†*Compare Pupo Shytti, Vice President of Albania, Mrs. P. Shittachitta, Mililani Town, Honolulu (Honolulu Star Bulletin), and Ms. Somchittindepata, Ithaca, N.Y. Dr. Sylvan Stool is a prominent Philadelphia surgeon, and Lotta Crap is the daughter of Paul Crap of Crap Bakery, Greencastle, Ind.*

‡*Compare Asia, Africa, America, and Europe Hamlin. Another brother, Hannibal, Vice President of the United States 1861 to 1865, nearly lost the election for Abraham Lincoln because his brother Africa was widely assumed to be black.*

Aurora Borealis Belsky*
  Staten Island, New York

Dr. Beaver†
  Obstetrician
  Falls Church, Virginia

Betty Burp
  (Bureau of Vital Statistics,
  Jacksonville, Florida)

Mr. Bones‡
  Undertaker
  Glasgow, Scotland

The Boring School§
  Boring, Oregon

*Compare Vernal Equinox Grossnickel, Blanchester, Ohio.

†Compare Dr. Fealy, gynecologist, West Palm Beach, Fla., and
Dr. Paternite, obstetrician, Akron, Ohio.

‡Compare Mole Funeral Home, Barnwell, Ga., and Human &
Pitt Funeral Services, Pretoria, South Africa. Sir Edward Pine-
Coffin was a Poor Relief Commissioner during the Irish potato
famine of 1844–45.

§Dr. Boring, dentist, plies his trade in St. Petersburg, Fla.,
while the Rev. Boring soothes his flock in the Bethel Alliance
Church in Sandusky, Ohio.

Aurora Borealis Belsky

Cheatham & Steele, Bankers

BUFORD PUSSER*
    Heroic Sheriff
    Selmer, Tennessee

DR. BULL†
    Pennsylvania State Secretary of Agriculture
    Philadelphia, Pennsylvania

BUSTER HYMEN
    (*San Francisco Examiner*)

CARDIAC ARREST DA SILVA
    Municipal Tax Collector
    Brazil
    (*Financial Times*)

CASHMERE TANGO OBEDIENCE‡
    Agriculturist
    Santa Cruz, California

CHEATHAM & STEELE, BANKERS§
    Wallowa County, Oregon

A suspicious car crash ended his career in 1977.

†*Subject of celebrated headline:* BULL TO SPEAK ON ARTIFICIAL INSEMINATION.

‡*Compare Clarence O. Bedient,* New York Times *ad salesman.*

§*The Office has a photograph of this establishment.*

CHERRI PANCAKE*
Curator, Museo Ixchel del Traje Indigena
Guatemala City, Guatemala

CHRIST T. SERAPHIM
Judge
Milwaukee, Wisconsin
(*United Press*)

(MRS.) CISTERN BROTHERS†
Hog Neck, North Carolina

MR. CLAPP‡
Venereal Disease Counselor and Lecturer
County Health Service
San Mateo, California

CLAUDE BALL§
Seattle, Washington
(*Seattle Post-Intelligencer*)

Compare Golden Pancake, Marion, Ohio.

†*Compare Knighton Day, New York City.*

‡*"Kept very busy indeed" by conditions in the late sixties.*

§*Compare Dr. Claude Organ, surgeon and director of Boys Town, Omaha, Nebr.*

CHIEF (CLAYTON) CROOK*
   Police Chief
   Brunswick, Ohio

C. MATHEWS DICK†
   Social Leader
   Newport, Rhode Island

COMFORT and SATISFY BOTTOM‡
   Sisters
   Wayne State University
   Detroit, Michigan

CONSTANT AGONY§
   Chazy Lake, New York

*A different Chief (Bernard) Crooke heads the Montgomery County, Md., police force. Narcissus Frett is Chief Confidential Investigator, Surrogate Court of Kings County, N.Y.

†Compare Dr. Dick, urologist, of Colorado Springs, Colo., and Adora Cox of Crapo, Md.

‡Compare Bump and Twinkle Quick, brother and sister, Sylvester, Ga.; also Silas Comfort Swallow, 1904 Prohibition party candidate for President, and Dreama Bottoms, Duke University, Durham, N.C.

§Compare Agonia Heimerdinger, Santa Ana, Calif.

REV. CORNELIUS WHUR*
Trashy Poet (1782–1853)
England

The Female Friend

In this imperfect, gloomy scene
Of complicated ill,
How rarely is a day serene,
The throbbing bosom still!
Will not a beauteous landscape bright
Or music's soothing sound,
Console the heart, afford delight,
And throw sweet peace around?
They may; but never comfort lend
Like an accomplished female friend.

With such a friend the social hour
In sweetest pleasure glides;
There is in female charms a power
Which lastingly abides;
The fragrance of the blushing rose,
Its tints and splendid hue,
Will with the season decompose,
And pass as flitting dew;
On firmer ties his joys depend
Who has a faithful female friend.

COTYS M. MOUSER
    Chief Clerk, U.S. Senate
    Committee on Agriculture and Forestry
    Washington, D.C.

CRYSTAL TOOT
    President, Kansas State PTA
    Great Bend, Kansas

C. SHARP MINOR*
    Silent Movie Organist
    Rochester, New York

CUPID RASH†
    England
    (*Western Morning News*)

*Compare O. Pinkypank, ukelele instructor, Sweet Springs, Mo.

†Father of nine; succeeded in getting eleven years behind in his rent before being evicted from public housing project.

DEMETRUS PLICK
   Interior Designer
   Boston, Massachusetts
   (Harvard Medical School *Alumni Bulletin*)

DR. & DR. DOCTOR*
   Westport, Connecticut

DOCTOR DOTTI†
   Psychiatrist
   Rome, Italy

EARLESS ROMERO
   Lafayette, Louisiana
   (Courthouse Records)

EASTER BUGGAGE‡
   New Orleans, Louisiana

One M.D. married another.

†*Husband of Audrey Hepburn. Compare Dr. Dement,
psychiatrist, Stanford University.*

‡*Recent offspring of Halloween Buggage. Compare Luscious
Easter, Euclid, Ohio, one of the first blacks to play for the
Cleveland Indians. A "big, fence-busting first baseman,"
recalled* Time *magazine.*

Demetrus Plick, Interior Designer

ECSTACY GOON
   (Wisconsin Historical Society,
   Madison, Wisconsin)

E. PLURIBUS EUBANKS*
   Longshoreman
   San Francisco, California

EUCALYPTUS YOHO
   Ashland Oil Dealer
   Portsmouth, Ohio

EVAN KEEL
   Goldsboro, North Carolina

DR. E. Z. FILLER
   Dentist
   Roslyn Heights, New York

FAIR HOOKER
   Football Player (End), for the
   Cleveland Browns
   Cleveland, Ohio

---

*Compare E. Pluribus Gass, Western Reserve University,
Cleveland, Ohio.

FAIRY CLUTTER
    Indiana University of Pennsylvania
    Women's Club
    Indiana, Pennsylvania

FANG W. WANG
    Mutual Fund Executive
    New York City

FANNY HUNNYBUN*
    Nanny
    South Devon, England

FAUNTLEROY SCHNAUZ
    (Educational Testing Service
    Princeton, New Jersey)

FEMALE JONES†
    University of Maryland Hospital
    Baltimore, Maryland

*Met and married Mr. Hunnybun, guest of employer. Died in
1975, aged ninety-seven.

†This not unusual given name — bestowed by hospitals in the
absence of a parental decision — is often pronounced fe-mà-le.
Compare Legitimate Jones and Male Infant Kilgore, both of
Detroit, Mich.

Felonious Fish

(Miss) Fishy Step*
  Pennsylvania

Fortunate Tarte
  Mary Fletcher Hospital,
  Burlington, Vermont

Rev. Fountain Wetmore Rainwater†
  Circuit-riding Preacher
  Kentucky

Dr. Gargle
  Dentist
  New York City‡

---

*Arrested for vagrancy. Compare Felonious Fish, Omaha, Nebr.,
and Halibut Justa Fish, Mastic, N.Y.

†Liked to sprint to church, read one verse from the Bible, and
sprint home. Compare Judith Moist.

‡Now retired to Florida. Dr. Toothaker, a dentist with the
Arizona Public Health Service, was killed by a rock fall while
visiting the Navajo National Monument. Dr. Pull practices
dentistry in St. Cloud, Minn., and Dr. Pulls at St. Mark's
Clinic, New York City.

GARNISH LURCH*
Railway Engineer
Jamaïca Government Railways
Jamaica

GINGER SCREWS CASANOVA†
Eureka, California
(*Eureka Times-Standard*)

GRETEL VON GARLIC‡
New York City

HADASSAH PECKER
Physician
New York City

At the throttle when a derailment killed 178 excursionists and injured several hundred more. (The Daily Gleaner, *1957, Kingston, Jamaica*)

†*Compare Mutual Screw Company, New York City.*

‡*Compare Ginger Clam, New York City, and Ingeborg von Zitzewitz.*

HANNIBAL TOTO*
Rome, Italy
(*London Daily Mail*)

HECTOR SPECTOR†
Royal Canadian Air Force

HEDDA HARE
Spring Valley, New York

HEIDI YUM-YUM GLUCK‡
Artist
Brooklyn, New York

HENRY FORD CARR§
Central City, Kentucky

*At a wedding, was requested to fire a salute; complied, using a shotgun, wounding the groom and twelve of the wedding guests.

†Compare Hubert Boobert, trombonist, Marion, Ohio, and Esther Pester.

‡Mr. Gluck père, infatuated by Gilbert and Sullivan, named his son Nanka, after Nanki-Poo, another character from The Mikado.

§Compare Iona Ford and (Mr.) Zeus Garage, industrial designer.

HENRY WILL BURST
  (*London Times Literary Supplement*)

HERMAN SHERMAN BERMAN*
  Commissioner of Deeds
  Bronx, New York

HILARIUS FUCHS†
  Continental Grain Company
  New York City

HOGJAW TWADDLE‡
  Morris Harvey College
  (now University of Charleston)
  Charleston, West Virginia

HONOR ROLL§
  Nurse-anesthetist
  Birmingham, Alabama

**Compare Wong Bong Fong of Hong Kong.* (Philadelphia Inquirer)

†*Compare Hilarious Conception, Hawaii.*

‡*Has found his name a valuable aid in breaking ice with new acquaintances. Compare Sianah E. Twaddle, San Mateo, Calif.*

§*Compare Charity Ball, Wichita, Kans.* (Wichita Eagle)

Hilarius Fuchs, Continental Grain Company

HORACE and BORIS MOROS*
   Brothers

IF-JESUS-CHRIST-HAD-NOT-DIED-FOR-THEE-
THOU-HADST-BEEN-DAMNED BAREBONES†
   London, England

IGNATZ DANGLE
   Grand Rapids Hospital,
   Grand Rapids, Michigan

ILONA SCHRECK-PUROLA‡
   Skin Pathologist
   (*Club* magazine)

IMMACULATE CONCEPTION FINKELSTEIN§
   New York Stock Exchange Investor

*Respectively, a New York City official and a Hollywood,
Calif., communist.*

†*Set up the first fire insurance office in Britain. Changed his
name to Nicholas Barbon.*

‡*Coauthoress,* Baldness and Its Cure.

§*South American customer of Oppenheimer & Co., New York
City. Compare Modest Newcomer Weisenburg, University of
California, Berkeley, Calif., and Jesus Christ Hooton, Cambridge,
Mass. (brother of Newton Hooton; both sons of Prof. Ernest
Hooton).*

I. M. Zamost
  Lawyer
  Highland Park, New Jersey

Ingeborg von Zitzewitz
  New York, New York

Iva Odor*
  Schoolteacher
  Spencer, Iowa

Ivan Karamanov†
  (*Maclean's Magazine*)

J. Fido Spot‡
  West Palm Beach, Florida

Compare Rev. Ivan Odor, Owosso, Mich.

†*Changed his name to John Dinkof Doikof. Pothuvilage Babyhamy,
changed her name in April 1974 to Ramya Briget Pothuvilage.*

‡*Mr. Spot has switched to an unlisted telephone number.
Compare Udo Pooch of Texas Agricultural and Mechanical
University, and Prof. J. C. Beaglehole, world authority on
Captain Cook.*

Kuhl Brieze

J. Minor Wisdom*
 Judge
 (*New York Times*)

John Hodge Opera House Centennial
Gargling Oil Samuel J. Tilden Ten Brook†
 Olcott, New York

John Wellborn Wallop‡
 University of California
 Berkeley, California

Mr. Joynt§
 Marijuana Analyst
 Royal Canadian Mounted Police Crime Lab.
 Alberta, Canada

Kuhl Brieze
 Palm Harbor, Florida

Compare Judge Judge, Second Judicial Dist., State of New York.

†*Born in 1876, the centennial year, and named in honor of John Hodge, who owned the Hodge Opera House, manufactured gargling oil, and supported the Presidential candidacy of Samuel J. Tilden. His friends called him "Buck." Compare Aldeberontophoscophonia Smith, Boston, Mass., and Pepsi Cola Atom-Bomb Washington, Upper Marlboro, Md. (youngest of twenty-two children).*

‡*Compare H. Wellborn Person.*

§*Christopher Logue, True Stories, London: A. P. Rushton, 1973.*

39

LAKE TROUT
    Attorney
    Los Angeles, California

LAVENDER HANKEY*
    Los Angeles, California

LEE BUM SUCK†
    Foreign Minister
    Seoul, South Korea

LEGRUNT E. CRAPPER‡
    Johns Hopkins Hospital
    Baltimore, Maryland
    (Harvard Medical School *Alumni Bulletin*)

---

*Compare Lacey Pantti, Republic, Mich. (*pronounced* punty).*

†Captain Robert E. Lee, U.S.N. (Ret.), noise monitor for the Montgomery County (Md.) Environmental Protection Department, changed his name to Roberto Edouardo Leon to qualify for "affirmative action" promotions ahead of his white peers. "Finding loopholes is my job," he said. "This is an insult to Hispanics," fumed the governor's Commissioner on Hispanic Affairs.

‡His doctor reports that his name may subsequently have been changed to LeGrant.

LESBIA LOBO*
Golfer

LOBELIA RUGTWIT HILDEBIDDLE
Psychology Student
Occidental College
Los Angeles, California

LOCH NESS HONTAS
Tulane University Medical School
New Orleans, Louisiana

LO FAT†
Retired Merchant Seaman
New York City

LOVEY NOOKEY GOOD‡
Texas State Health Department
Austin, Texas

*Winner of the 1953 Broadmoor Ladies Invitational Golf Tournament in Colorado Springs, Colo.

†Compare Shark Ho, New York City.

‡Compare Cassandra Nookiesnatch (possibly of Eskimo origin).

MAGDALENA BABBLEJACK
(*Maclean's Magazine*)

MAJOR QUAINTANCE
U.S. Army
(*The New Yorker*)

MARMALADE P. VESTIBULE
Door-to-door Firewood Salesman
Cambridge, Massachusetts

MEMORY LEAKE
Contractor
Tupelo, Mississippi

(MISS) MIGNON HAMBURGER
University of Wisconsin
Madison, Wisconsin

MING-TOY EPSTEIN*
New York City

MINNIE MAGAZINE
Editor, *Time* magazine
New York City

Long questioned by the Office, Ming-Toy's authenticity has been established by S. J. Perelman and others.

Minnie Magazine, Magazine Editor

Needa Climax
    Methodist Church Officer
    Centerville, Louisiana

Never Fail*
    Builder
    Tulsa, Oklahoma

Noble Puffer†
    Superintendent of Schools
    Cook County, Illinois

Noel T. Tweet
    (*Business Week*)

Nosmo King‡
    Pikesville, Maryland

*Mrs. Never Fail, exasperated by her husband's accounts of his achievements with "beautiful blondes," finally sought divorce. (Associated Press)

†Compare Noble Tickle, Rating, Royal Navy.

‡Named for sign in waiting room of Dr. Brull, Sugarcane Road, Pikesville.

NOVICE FAWCETT
>President, Ohio State University
>Columbus, Ohio

NOWAY NEAR WHITE
>Shoe Salesman
>Columbus, Ohio

ODIOUS CHAMPAGNE*
>Paper Mill Employee
>Winslow, Maine

OLDMOUSE WALTZ
>Federal Writers Project
>New Orleans, Louisiana

OOFTY GOOFTY BOWMAN
>Shakespearean Actor
>Milwaukee, Wisconsin
>(*Milwaukee Sentinel*)

OPHELIA BUMPS†
>Richmond, Virginia

Compare Romeo Q. Champagne, state official, N.H.

†*Reported by hospital where she was a patient. Compare
Ophelia Tittey, Fall River, Mass.*

Oscar Asparagus, Basketball Star

FATHER O'PRAY*
  Church of St. Ignatius Loyola
  New York City

OSCAR ASPARAGUS
  Basketball Star
  (*Maclean's Magazine*)

PAFIA PIFIA PEFIA POFIA PUFIA DA COSTA
  Brazil
  (*Financial Times*)

PEARL HARBOR
  Telephone Operator of the *Birmingham News*
  Birmingham, Alabama

PETER BETER†
  Attorney
  Washington, D.C.

*Compare Rev. Goodness, Church of the Ascension, New York City.

†Pronounced beeter. Perennial unsuccessful candidate for governor of West Virginia.

PHILI B. DEBOO*
   Professor of Geology
   Memphis, Tennessee

PHILOMENA CUNEGUNDE WEWE†
   Hawaii

(MISS) PINK GASH
   Hendersonville, North Carolina
   (*The Saturday Review*)

PIROUETTE SPIEGEL
   White House Staff‡
   Washington, D.C.

(MISS) PTARMIGAN TEALE§
   Boston, Massachusetts

Compare Philander Philpott Pettibone (Maclean's Magazine).

†*Compare Steven Weewee, Indiana University student.*

‡*During Kennedy Administration.*

§*Daughter of E. W. Teale, naturalist. Compare (Mrs.) Birdie Peacock, Goldsboro, N.C.*

RADICAL LOVE*
   Selective Service Registrant
   Washington, D.C.

RAPER YOWLER
   Dayton, Ohio

ROMAN PRETZEL†
   Tel Aviv, Israel

ROOSEVELT CABBAGESTALK‡
   Pittsburgh, Pennsylvania
   (*Philadelphia Inquirer*, quoting
   Advertising Age)

ROSEY and DEWEY BUTT§
   Sister and Brother
   Peru, Indiana

*Compare Love Newlove, Toronto, Ont. Natania Schitlove
changed her name to Laura Schitlove.*

†*A frequent correspondent in the* Jerusalem Post.

‡*Compare Zeditha Cabbagestalk, Safeway cashier, Washington,*
D.C.

§*Compare Rose Rump, Bettendorf, Iowa, and Rosie Rump, San
Francisco, Calif.; also Barbara Fatt Heine, New York City.*
(New York Times)

Rosey Vice*
   Multiple Larcenist
   Great Glemham
   Suffolk, England

Rosy Yass†
   Cincinnati, Ohio

Dr. Safety First
   Tulsa, Oklahoma

Sandwith Drinker
   Class of '71
   University of Pennsylvania

Sara Struggles Nicely
   Clearwater, Florida
   (*Cleveland Plain Dealer*)

Possessed of a notable "green thumb," she was released from confinement each spring to assist in planting.

†So taken with her maiden name that after marriage she continued to maintain a separate telephone directory listing for it.

Sandwith Drinker

Commander Sink, U.S.N.

SERIOUS MISCONDUCT*
   Welwyn, England

SHLOMO TURTLEDOVE
   Tel Aviv, Israel

COMMANDER SINK, U.S.N.
   Fort Washington, Maryland

SOLOMON GEMORAH
   Brooklyn, New York

(MISS) SUE YU
   Library Card Holder
   Flushing, New York

TARANTULA TURNER
   New Orleans, Louisiana

TAURA LOURA GOLDFARB
   New York City

T. FUD PUCKER TUCKER
   Bountiful, Utah

*Compare General Error, Pueblo, Colo.

Mrs T. Picnick, nutritionist

MRS. THERESA PICNICK*
    Nutritionist
    Worcester, Massachusetts

TOPPIE SMELLIE
    T.V. Chicken Coating Mix Endorser

URBAN SHOCKER
    Pitcher, New York Yankees
    New York City

URE A. PIGG†
    Restaurateur
    Portland, Oregon
    (*Oregon Journal*)

URINE MCZEAL‡
    Washington County, Florida

Compare Bacon Chow, nutritionist, Johns Hopkins School of Public Health, Baltimore, Md.

†*Compare Ima Hogg, civic leader, Houston, Tex. Ura Hogg is a myth.*

‡*Compare Argo Pisson, Quality Control Engineer, Raytheon Corporation, Lexington, Mass.; also Kitty Peed, Cape Coral, Fla.*

Ursula Woop
National Typewriting Champion
East Germany

U. S. Bond*
Safe Deposit Manager
Harvard Trust Company
Cambridge, Massachusetts

Vaseline Love†
Jackson, Tennessee

Professor Verbal Snook
Chairman, Mathematics Department
Oral Roberts University
Tulsa, Oklahoma

Vile Albert
St. Johnsbury, Vermont

*Compare President Overcash of American Credit Corporation, Dallas, Tex.

†Compare Love Kisses Love, mess attendant, U.S.S. Lexington, and Vaseline Maleria.

Vile Albert

Void Null

Void Null*
    Schoolteacher
    San Diego, California

Wambly Bald
    Reporter, *New York Post*
    New York City

Zilpher Spittle
    English parish record
    (*Maclean's Magazine*)

Zowie Bowie†
    (*London Times Literary Supplement*)

Born January 3, 1904, in Mexico, Mo., to Henrietta and Thomas Jefferson Null, whose occupation is enigmatically given as "panatorium."

†*Son of rock singer.*

Acknowledgments

The Office of Nomenclature Stabilization expresses particular gratitude to Louisa Spencer, who checked the entries, to Timothy Dickinson, quenchless fount of esoterica, and to our wife, Francie. Also to valued correspondents Charles Francis Adams, Calvin Anderson, Robert Armistead, Norman R. Atwood, Bernard M. Axelrod, The Rev. Paul C. Bailey, Shirley Barstow, Miss Iris Bass, Robert L. Bates, Shirley Bean, T. O. Beidelman, Toby Bellin, Phenix Benton, Richard J. Blume, Mary Jemail Brady, Bruce Bratton, William Brock Jr., J. S. Bryan III, Warren Buffett, Mrs. William R. Bullard, Barbara Burkart, Nancy Butler, Robert J. Cahn, Mrs. Dorcas Capito, Steve Carper, J. A. Casserly, David Chadwick-Brown, Lynn Chalmers, Harry B. Chase, Jr., Dorothy R. Chmela, Dr. Milton M. Conliffe, Clara Conoboy, Nan Coppock-Bland, J. H. Coulter, Bill Crowe, Jane Cunningham, Mrs. Kay E. Delaney, Wayne E. Duncan, Linda DuVal, Anita B. Egan, David P. Fairchild, Mrs. Walter L. Feibelman, Michael Flanigan, Roy Foster, Stephen Foster, Angeline B. Frost, Mrs. John W. Garland, E. Faye Geidl, Mr. & Mrs. Clyde Gilmour, Mrs. John R. Ginger, Margaret S. Good, Al Gorisek, Rhoda Granat, Alastair Grant, Donald Gray, Mrs. Vida-Wynne Griffin, Alix Gross, Cortland Hamilton, Anthony Hass, E. Parker Hayden, Jr., Mrs. Thomasine Haynes, R. Herreid, Robert Hinklin, P. J. Hoff, Margaret E. Holm, Alix Hornblower, Patricia Huber-Brown, Thomas Jackson, Dennis F. Jensen, Mrs. David Jones, Joseph Kane, Jeanette B. Katz,

Al Key, Charles Krebs, Edward B. Larner, Elizabeth Lee, Herman R. Leider, Leon Levy, Christopher Logue, Robert McCaig, Robert McCurdy, Jo Manning, Harry Mathews, Francois Mignon, Donna Mobley, the staff of the Montgomery County (Ohio) Historical Society, Mrs. Edward B. Morris, Ruth R. Nadell, Jane Navarre, W. Jack Neff, Deborah Neustetter, John Newlove, Thomas D. Nicholson, John Otruba, Dan Ottinger, Hanna Papanek, David G. Park, John Parkinson III, Ruth M. Parmelee, Arthur H. Parsons, Claiborne Pell, Jack Pement, Douglas Pennoyer, S. J. Perelman, Pinkie Perry, Tony Phillips, George Plimpton, Marilyn G. Putz, Ann Rice, Dr. Winston P. Riehl, Cornelius van S. Roosevelt, Dr. Stephen D. Rosenbaum, G. Rosenfield, Babette Rosmond, Patrica Ryan, Michael Scharfman, Shirley Schodowsky, Mrs. Jules Schrager, Mrs. Reed B. Sheffield, Mrs. Lyndon F. Small, Mrs. Dudley H. Smith, Henry Ladd Smith, J. Andrew Squires, Mrs. Ethel Strangewood, Dr. A. Bradley Soule, Barry Talesnick, Nina Train, Patrolman Jim Triano, Mrs. H. E. Tompkins, Joan B. True, Judge Richard J. Wallach, Dr. William Waring, Mrs. Judith P. Weissman, Gail White, Mrs. Halle Wise, Clement B. Wood, Robert B. Wright, Judge Don Young, Kenn Young and Isidore M. Zamost.

Index of Family Names

Designed by Katy Homans
Type set in Monotype Dante by Michael & Winifred Bixler